Leopards

Patricia Kendell

HODDER
Wayland

An imprint of Hodder Children's Books

Alligators Chimpanzees Dolphins Elephants
Gorillas Grizzly Bears Leopards Lions
Pandas Polar Bears Sharks Tigers

© 2003 White-Thomson Publishing Ltd

Produced for Hodder Wayland by White-Thomson Publishing Ltd

Editor: Kay Barnham
Designer: Tim Mayer
Consultant: Callum Rankine – International Species Officer at WWF-UK
Language Consultant: Norah Granger – Senior Lecturer in Primary Education at the University of Brighton
Picture research: Shelley Noronha – Glass Onion Pictures

Published in Great Britain in 2003 by Hodder Wayland, an imprint of Hodder Children's Books.

Photograph acknowledgements:
Anup Shah/naturepl.com 11; Bruce Coleman cover & 4 (Alain Compost), 25 (Rod Williams), 28; Ecoscene 24 (Robert Baldwin), 21 (E J Bent), 22 (Lindegger), 17 (Kjell Sandved); FLPA 26 (Michael Gore), 9, 10 (Mark Newman), 5 (Philip Perry), 7 (Fritz Polking), 13 & 32 (Sunset); NHPA 8 (J & A Scott); OSF 14-15 (Daniel Cox), 27 (Colin Monteath), 19 (Richard Packwood), 6 (Mary Plage), 20 (Rafi Ben-Shahar), 12 (Steve Turner); Science Photo Library 18, 23 (Peter Chadwick), 29 (Gregory Dimijian); WTPix 16 (Steve White-Thomson).

British Library Cataloguing in Publication Data
Kendell, Patricia
  Leopard. – (In the wild)
  1. Leopard – Juvenile literature
  I. Title II. Barnham, Kay
  599.7'554

ISBN: 0 7502 4129 2

Printed in Hong Kong by Wing King Tong Co. Ltd.

Hodder Children's Books
A division of Hodder Headline Limited
338 Euston Road, London NW1 3BH

Produced in association with WWF-UK.
WWF-UK registered charity number 1081247.
A company limited by guarantee number 4016725.
Panda device © 1986 WWF ® WWF registered trademark owner.

Contents

Where leopards live — 4

Baby leopards — 6

Looking after the cubs — 8

Growing up — 10

Leaving home — 12

On the move — 14

Food — 16

Out of sight — 18

Hunting — 20

Night and day — 22

Threats... — 24

... and dangers — 26

Helping leopards to survive — 28

Further information — 30

Glossary — 31

Index — 32

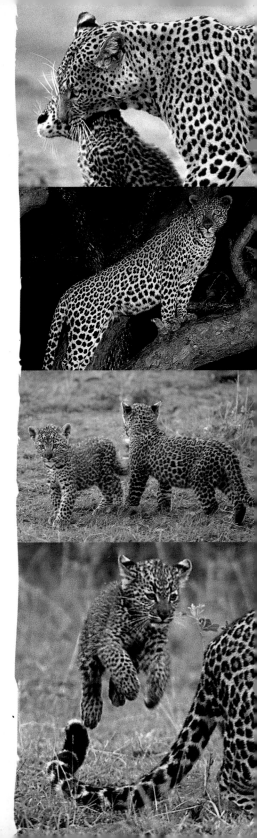

Where leopards live

Leopards can be found in parts of Africa and Asia. They are able to live in many different places such as grasslands or in the **rainforest**.

Some leopards survive even in **desert** places.

Baby leopards

Two or three **cubs** are born in a safe **den**.
Newborn cubs are tiny and helpless.

They stay close to their mother, drinking
her milk to grow big and strong.

Looking after the cubs

Mother leopards keep their cubs clean
by licking them all over.

If there is danger, a mother leopard will gently
carry the cubs to a safer place.

Growing up

When they are eight weeks old,
the cubs leave the den.

As they grow older, the cubs learn how to hunt by playing at pouncing on their mother's tail.

Leaving home

The young leopards leave their mother when they are about two years old.

Once they are grown up, leopards live alone in a **territory** of their own. They only come together to **mate**.

On the move

Like all big cats, leopards can run and jump easily and **gracefully**.

This snow leopard is leaping over rocks in its mountain home in Asia.

Food

Leopards will kill and eat many different kinds of animal in their territory, like these **impala** and zebra.

Leopards' powerful chests and front legs help
them to climb trees easily. They often drag their
prey up a tree, out of reach of other animals.

Out of sight

The pattern and colour of a leopard's fur
makes it hard for prey animals to spot it.

Leopards have long whiskers to help them feel their way when it gets dark.

Hunting

Most leopards hunt at night. Some creep up
and pounce on their prey.

Other leopards climb trees and wait for animals
to pass by. Then they jump down on to their prey.

Night and day

Leopards are active mainly at night.
They can see very well in the dark.

They usually sleep all day in a tree, especially
if it is hot, or after they have eaten a big meal.

Threats...

It is against the law to hunt leopards, but some people kill them and sell their fur.

Today, there are very few Persian leopards left because too many of them have been hunted for their beautiful fur.

... and dangers

People are cutting down trees and taking the leopards' territory to grow food.

When people live in leopard territory, the leopards have less food. Herders protect their animals from attack and sometimes kill hungry snow leopards.

Helping leopards to survive

Tourists will pay to see animals in the wild.
This is one way that local people can earn
money without killing leopards.

If people look after the forests and mountains, and find ways of sharing them with leopards, then more leopards will survive in the future.

Further information

Find out more about how we can help leopards in the future.

ORGANIZATIONS TO CONTACT

WWF-UK
Panda House, Weyside Park,
Godalming, Surrey GU7 1XR
Tel: 01483 426444
Website: http://www.wwf.org

International Snow Leopard Trust
4649 Sunnyside Avenue North,
Suite 325
Seattle, Washington 98103
USA
Tel: 00 206 632 2421
Website: http://www.snowleopard.org

Cat Specialist Group
The World Conservation Union (IUCN)
1172 Bougy
Switzerland
Tel: 0041 21 808 6012
Website: http://lynx.uio.no/lynx/catfolk

BOOKS

Leopards: Spotted Hunters (Wild World of Animals): Lola Schaefer, Capstone Press 2001.

The Snow Leopard: Tessa Radcliffe, Puffin 1996.

Wild cats (Know-it-alls): Diana Muldrow, Learning Horizons 1998.

Why the Leopard has Spots: Katherine Mead, Raintree Steck-Vaughn 1997.

Big Cats (Nature Watch): Heinemann

Leopard (Natural World): Bill Jordan, Hodder Wayland 2001.

Glossary

WEBSITES

Most young children will need adult help when visiting websites. Those listed have child-friendly pages to bookmark.

http://www.leopardsetc.com/meet.html
Children can hear the leopards roar and find out about them in text and photographs.

http://www.kidsplanet.org/factsheets/snow_leopard.html
This website provides information about, and photographs of, snow leopards.

http://snowleopard.org/islt/classroom
This website has quizzes, games and slide shows. There is also information about how children can help the endangered snow leopard.

cubs – the name for baby leopards.

den – a wild animal's home.

desert – a very dry place where few trees grow.

graceful – to move in a smooth, flowing way.

impala – a small deer.

mate – when male and female leopards come together to make babies.

prey – an animal hunted by another animal for food.

rainforest – forests in hot, wet places.

territory – the home area of an animal.

Index

C
climb 15, 17, 21
cubs 6, 8, 9, 10, 11

D
den 6, 10
drink 7

E
eat 16, 23

F
fur 18, 24, 25

H
hunt 11, 20, 24, 25

J
jump 14, 21

K
kill 16, 24, 27, 28

M
mate 13
milk 7
mother 7, 8, 9, 11, 12

P
prey 17, 18, 20, 21

R
run 14

S
see 22
sleep 23

T
tourists 28
trees 15, 17, 21, 23, 26

W
whiskers 19